Lynette Woodard

By
Matthew Newman

Edited By
Dr. Howard Schroeder
Professor in Reading and Language Arts
Dept. of Elementary Education
Mankato State University

Produced & Designed By

Baker Street Productions, Ltd.

*Special thanks
to Coach Duane Schmidt
and Wichita North High School*

CRESTWOOD HOUSE
**Mankato, Minnesota
U.S.A.**

LIBRARY OF CONGRESS CATALOGING-IN-PUBLICATION DATA

Newman, Matthew.
  Lynette Woodard.

(SCU-2)
SUMMARY: Traces the life and career of the individual who made sports history by becoming the first woman to play basketball for the Harlem Globetrotters.
  1. Woodard, Lynette — Juvenile literature. 2. Basketball players — United States — Biography — Juvenile literature. 3. Harlem Globetrotters — Juvenile literature. (1. Woodard, Lynette. 2. Women basketball players. 3. Basketball players. 4. Afro-Americans — Biography) I. Schroeder, Howard. II. Title.
GV884.W63N49   1986   796.32'3'0924   (B)   (92)   86-19737
ISBN 0-89686-316-6

International Standard Book Number:	Library of Congress Catalog Card Number:
0-89686-316-6	86-19737

PHOTO CREDITS

John Iacono/Sports Illustrated: 5, 28, 32-33, 34-35, 40-41, 44-45
UPI/Bettmann Newsphotos: 6
Focus On Sports: 9, 30-31, 38-39, 46-47
Kansas University: 14, 18, 22
Heinz Kluetmeier/Sports Illustrated: 16
Rich Clarkson/Sports Illustrated: 21
AP/Wide World: 24-25, 27, 43
Joshua Touster/Sports Chrome: 37

CRESTWOOD HOUSE
Hwy. 66 South Box 3427
Mankato, MN 56002-3427

TABLE OF CONTENTS

THE FIRST FEMALE GLOBETROTTER

On October 16, 1985, the Harlem Globetrotters opened their season in Brisbane, Australia. The newest Globetrotter, Lynette Woodard, waited in her dressing room moments before the game. She put three tri-colored bands on each wrist. She also put on the famous star-studded Globetrotter jersey. Then she went over the team's special routines once more in her mind.

In the arena, a full house waited for the team to take the floor. For basketball fans, a Globetrotters' game is always a special event. This game was even more so. Fans were about to see history in the making. Shortly, Lynette Woodard would become the first woman ever to play basketball along side men in a professional game.

For Lynette, it was a moment for which she had long waited. "It was in my heart," she said. "My cousin, Geese Ausbie, had played for the Globetrotters. Every time they came to town, I was fascinated by the things I saw them do. When you play basketball, you go on the court and fantasize about being different players. The Globetrotters were the team I thought about all the time."

When Lynette was in college, she once wrote to her cousin about wanting to play for the Globetrotters. Her cousin did not give her much hope at the time. In 1985, however, Lynette and twenty other female players were invited to try out for the team. The Globetrotters thought a woman would make more people come to their games. All of the women saw it as a once-in-a-lifetime chance.

Lynette Woodard is the first female Globetrotter.

Lynette competed with the best to become the first lady Globetrotter.

"Everyone there was shocked," Lynette recalls. "The play was incredible. I've never seen anything like it, not even at the Olympic trials. There was some of the greatest basketball going on."

In the end, Lynette was chosen above the others. Lynette's ball-handling skills and "extra charisma" made the difference, according to Globetrotters' coach Larry Rivers.

In Brisbane, Lynette entered the game in the second

quarter. She took part in the crowd-pleasing "Globetrotter Weave," in which three players move in a figure-eight pattern around another player doing ball stunts in the middle. All kidding aside, Lynette knew she was setting a new milestone. From that moment on, no one could say women did not have the skills to play on a professional level.

At the same time, Lynette also became part of the Globetrotters' own unique history. Over thirty years, the Globetrotters have played before 100 million fans. They are the world's most famous basketball team. And no matter what language is spoken where they play, the team's positive message always comes through.

"They're a very special group," Lynette says. "You know, the Globetrotters are known for their warm-heartedness, and that didn't just come about. That's their personality and they treat me with the same warmness and respect they give each other."

During the next year, Lynette would play 173 games in 141 cities across the globe. In every arena, fans greeted her warmly. Overall, attendance for the games rose thirty percent. It was just a reward for the Globetrotters. Years ago, the Globetrotters led the way in giving black males a chance to play before the NBA did.

Lynette hopes that history will repeat itself. "I don't know how long it will take," she says, "but a woman will play in the NBA. I want people to see me play with the Globetrotters and say a woman could also have the ability to play in the NBA."

GROWING UP IN WICHITA, KANSAS

Lynette Woodard was born on August 12, 1959. She was raised along with one brother and one sister in Wichita, Kansas. Lynette's mother, Dorothy Woodard, was a homemaker. Lynette's father, Lugene, was a firefighter.

When Lynette was five, a tragedy took place near the Woodard home. An Air Force tank plane crashed just a short distance away. Fourteen homes were destroyed. Thirty people died. Seconds after the crash, Lynette stood in a neighbor's yard and watched another house burn to the ground.

"I realize now that it was the first thing that I remember," Lynette says. "I can remember just everything going so fast. I was at a neighbor's house . . . and I saw all this smoke. This house just burst into fire . . . and somebody took me away.

"I guess the mind has a way of telling you, 'Hey, this is important!' "

When Lynette was ten, the city built a basketball court on the crash site. Lynette and her brother Darrell began spending hours on the court shooting hoops. "Until then," Lynette says, "my brother Darrell and I just tore up our room playing ball with balled up paper or socks. So my mom was really happy to see that park."

Lynette got into the habit of playing basketball year-round. Most of the time she played with boys. "All the

Lynette has played basketball with men since she was a teenager.

girls were older," Lynette explains. "They didn't really want me around."

The boys found out that Lynette could more than hold her own on the court. And they didn't really have to drag her out to play, either. "I was always looking for a chance to play," Lynette recalls. "Soon guys were choosing me before their friends. Or I would be doing the choosing."

When Lynette entered the ninth grade at Marshall Junior High, she joined the girls' basketball team. She became known as one of the best one-on-one players around. One day, Duane Schmidt came to watch Lynette play. Schmidt was the girls basketball coach at Wichita North High School. He asked if Lynette would be interested in joining the Wichita North junior varsity. Lynette politely turned down the offer. In her mind, she felt she was already good enough to play for the varsity. A year later, Coach Schmidt came to agree with her.

THE WICHITA NORTH HIGH SCHOOL LEGEND

In the year before Lynette joined the Wichita North Redskins, the team's record was 0-8. Some said the Redskins were one of the worst teams in the city. In fact, Coach Schmidt had trouble getting good teams to agree to play them.

In 1974-75, however, the other teams wanted to avoid the Redskins for a different reason. The Redskins' new star, 5'11", 155-pound Lynette Woodard, had turned the team into a powerhouse. That year, the Redskins had a 13-1 record. Woodard averaged 25.5 points each game. She led the team in scoring in every game but one.

At the end of the year, Wichita North played Centralia for the 5-A State crown. Over 2,500 fans came out to watch the two best girls basketball teams square off. With only 2:52 left in the game, the two teams were tied. Moments later, after Woodard gave out two assists, got a rebound, and scored, it was all over. The final tally was 68-64, in favor of Wichita North. This gave the Redskins their first 5-A State Title.

In 1975-76, the Redskins picked up where they had left off. They won nineteen games in a row over a two-year period. By season's end, Lynette had piled up 384 points. Wichita North won the City League Championship. The team's only setback was a four-point loss to Hutchinson in the 5-A State final.

THE LAST-SECOND SHOT

In two years, the Wichita North Redskins had a 36-2 record. Lynette had high hopes for her final season. "I'm excited about basketball more than I have been," she said. "This is my last year, so I want to make it my best."

In the very first game of her senior season, Lynette showed that she had yet to reach her peak on the court. In an amazing one-woman show, Lynette had 50 points, 16 rebounds, and 13 steals. The final score: Lynette Woodard 77, Derby High 16.

By the end of the year, it became clear that no one player — no one team even — could stop Lynette on the court. Fans had never seen anyone quite like her. For the season, Lynette averaged over 33 points and 20 rebounds a game.

In a replay of the year before, Wichita North met Hutchinson in the 5-A State title game. Once again, the outcome of the game was in doubt right up until the final seconds. With only a few seconds left on the clock, the Redskins trailed by a point. Coach Schmidt called a timeout to map out strategy. Everyone in the building already knew, however, who would be getting the ball.

When Lynette got the inbounds pass, she dribbled the length of the floor through a maze of defenders. Then, with only a second left on the clock, she went up from twelve feet away. The ball went in, tried to come out, and went back in again. The buzzer sounded. Victory!

"I was praying it would go in," Lynette said later. "I had faith in it. This is the one I really wanted. I always said the game isn't over until the final buzzer."

After the season, Lynette was named as 5-A High School Player of the Year. She was also named as a starter on *Parade* magazine's all-America team. In three years she had led the Redskins to a 59-3 record. More than anyone, she had helped to put girls' basketball "on the map."

"When I first started playing for North, no one really attended the games," Lynette said. "Now you have as many people at the girls' games, as you have at the boys'. I think that women athletes have more to look forward to, such as scholarships to attend colleges. They can also look forward to international competition and the Olympics."

THE ALL-AMERICAN JAYHAWK

After graduation, Lynette tried to decide which college she wanted to attend. She had gotten over one hundred scholarship offers, but had no way to visit the schools. At the time, females had to pay their own way to visit each campus.

"I had all kinds of offers, but I didn't really go take a look at any school," Lynette says. "You have to pay your own way to visit schools. It's not like the men."

Lynette wanted a school with high academics as well as a good basketball program. In the end, she chose Kansas University (KU). "I didn't really want to go to Kansas," Lynette said at the time. "I felt it was almost like not leaving home."

After a short while, Lynette knew she had made the right choice. Lynette's new basketball coach, Marian Washington, saw that there were ways that even a great player like Lynette could improve her skills. Coach Washington did not coddle Lynette and was tougher on her than Lynette expected. She knew this would bring out the best in Lynette.

In her first season, Lynette showed she could handle the higher level of play in college. In the early season Lady Jayhawk Classic, Lynette had 31 points and 33 rebounds. For the season, she scored 30 points or more six times. Lynette's 14.8 rebound average led the nation. The KU team finished with its best record ever, at 22-11.

By the end of the season, Lady Jayhawk fans were flocking to the games. Lynette's court style mixed speed, grace, and power. The result was pure magic.

"Sometimes I know what I'm doing, other times I just see an opening and move in," Lynette said in describing her amazing "moves" on the court.

Lynette chose to attend Kansas University, so she could get a good education, as well as play basketball.

In honor of her efforts in 1977-78, *Street and Smith* named Lynette as Freshman of the Year. She also became only the third freshman ever to be named to the women's All-America team.

"I just wanted to play my best for the school," Lynette said. "I never thought I could make the team my first year .... To me, this is enough to make me feel like I have to put another one hundred percent into my game next year. I'll just keep saying: 'You can make it ... you can make it . .. you can make it.' "

THE UNITED STATES' NATIONAL BASKETBALL TEAM

In 1976, when Lynette was still playing for Wichita North High School, she thought about going out for the U.S. Olympic team. In order to do so, however, she would have had to miss too much school. Instead, Lynette watched the women's team win a silver medal.

"I watched them on television and I guess I was expecting them to be superhuman," Lynette recalls. "But they really didn't impress me."

After her freshman year at KU, Lynette joined the U.S. National Women's Basketball Team. This team played other amateur squads in Japan and China. Lynette averaged 10 points a game in twelve contests.

"We had twelve games and won three," Lynette

Lynette played basketball for the U.S. National Women's Basketball team in 1978.

remembers. "The team was down about it, but we played Olympic teams from Russia, Japan, and China. They all have played together ten to twelve years and were a lot older than we were."

Despite their losses, the U.S. team hoped to gain by playing against teams they might face later on in the Olympics. Of all the foreign teams, the Russian women were the most feared.

"Russia was the toughest game," Lynette says. "We got blown away, but we were the only team to hold them below one hundred points."

THE WORLD UNIVERSITY GAMES

In the fall of 1978-79, Lynette was named co-captain of the Lady Jayhawks. The team had another great season, finishing at 30-8. In the AIAW (Association for Intercollegiate Athletics for Women) post-season tournament, KU was beaten by Louisiana Tech, 100-61.

During the season, Lynette became the first KU player ever to score over a thousand points (1,177) in one year. This was more points scored during a season than any player — male or female — in the nation. Her scoring average was 31.7 points per game. Lynette's defense was also first-rate. Her quick hands gathered 193 steals, the top figure for all female players.

In the summer, Lynette once again played for the U.S.

National Team. The highlight of the team's tour took place in the World University Games, held in Mexico City, Mexico. Few gave the U.S. team much of a chance in the tournament. For one thing, the same teams had already beaten the U.S. a year earlier. Beyond this, the U.S. had yet to beat the Russians in over thirty years of play.

After four games, the U.S. team was the surprise of the tournament. With four straight wins, only two teams —Russia and Cuba — stood in the way for the gold medal. When the U.S. team met the Soviets, the score went back and forth all game long. With only fifty seconds left, the Soviets trailed and held the ball for one final shot. A Russian player shot — and missed! The U.S. team held on for an 83-81 victory.

In the title game against Cuba, Lynette scored 19 points to help the U.S. women's team earn it's first gold medal in many years.

THE JAYHAWKS' "LEAPIN' LIZARD"

As a fulltime athlete, Lynette was used to life at a fast pace. She spent a lot of time in the gym and on the road playing basketball. But Lynette was also a fulltime student, and very active in her church. Most people were amazed by her energy. She always found time to help a friend or classmate. Lynette took pride in proving that a world-class athlete could be a world-class person, too.

In 1979-80, Lynette became a junior at KU. At this point, she was well on her way towards a degree in communications. She had a high B average in her courses. At the end of the year, Lynette was named as an Academic all-American. This special honor goes to athletes who excel in the classroom as well as in the gym.

On the basketball court, Lynette took on a whole new role with the Lady Jayhawks. In her first two years, she had usually played the forward position. As a junior, Lynette was moved to guard. As the team's leading ball-handler, Lynette had to tap a wide range of skills. One of her jobs was to move the ball quickly up the court. If a teammate was open, Lynette had to be willing to give up the ball. To someone used to carrying the scoring load, this isn't always easy to accept. To Lynette, however, it was worth doing if it helped the team.

"I'm learning the feel of the ball a lot better," she said. "And that makes my shot better.

"I've never played guard before. It's always been a

In 1979, Lynette helped the U.S. women's team to earn its first gold medal in many years.

19

dream. But I always played some other position because of my height."

In truth, many big players like to fancy themselves as ballhandlers. They like the idea that they can be subtle as well as forceful. In Lynette's case, however, this was more than wishful thinking. Her range of skills seemed to go well beyond those of the normal "big" player's. She could glide through traffic or pop a long jump shot. She could drive the length of the floor or soar for rebounds. In fact, her teammates nicknamed her the 'Leapin' Lizard' because of her wide range of skills.

As a junior, Lynette once again led the Lady Jayhawks into the post-season AIAW tournament. They got closer, but still lost again to Louisiana Tech, 81-73, in the AIAW Sectionals.

Lynette averaged 23.8 points and 10.5 rebounds for the season. For the second year in a row, she led the nation in steals with 177. The Lady Jayhawks finished with a 28-9 record, ninth-ranked in the country. After the season, Lynette was named to the Kodak All-America team for the third year in a row.

THE 1980 OLYMPIC TEAM

In 1980, Lynette was one of 183 females invited to tryout for the women's U.S. Olympic basketball team. The tryouts were held over five days in Colorado Springs, Colorado. Lynette worked harder than ever to show her

In 1980, Lynette tried out for the U.S. Olympic basketball team.

Lynette worked hard and was chosen to be one of twelve players on the U.S. team.

skills. To her, making the Olympic team was a lifelong goal. "It's the ultimate in amateur sports," she said.

At first, Olympic coach Pat Head Summit had doubts about whether Woodard could help the U.S. team. She didn't doubt Lynette's one-on-one skills. Coach Summit wondered though, if Woodard could play within a team concept. In Lynette's own words, her system had always simply been to "go to the hoop."

In the end, Woodard proved too talented to ignore. Coach Summit saw that Lynette was willing to try to adapt her style. After the tryouts, Lynette was one of only twelve players chosen for the U.S. team.

The Olympic games were to be held in Moscow, Russia that year. Before the games could begin, however, U.S. President Carter ordered a boycott. This meant that Lynette, along with her teammates, could not compete. Despite the setback, Lynette still saw the bright side.

"At least I got to play in a pre-Olympic tournament in Bulgaria," she said. "So many people trained . . . and never received a chance to exhibit their worth."

THE ALL-TIME SCORING QUEEN

By the middle of her senior season at KU, Lynette was nearing an all-time scoring record. Going into a game against Stephen Austin College, Lynette had 3,204 points in just under four years of play. This put Lynette in a tie

*Lynette shows off some of the ball-handling skills she
learned while playing at Kansas.*

with Cindy Broglin for the most points scored by a female at the Division I level.

Lynette needed less than a minute to break the old record. With a twelve-foot jumper, Lynette put her name at the top of the all-time scoring list. For the rest of the season, every point she scored added to her record total.

"I'm glad it happened early," Lynette said. "I'm glad it was only one point. I was really nervous tonight. I didn't realize how nervous I was."

THE FIRST FEMALE DUNK

With the all-time scoring record in hand, Lynette set her sights on a special "goal." She wanted to become the first woman ever to "dunk" a basketball in an official game. "I can't believe no woman can do it," Lynette said. "But I know when it's done, by me or anyone else, it will change the game. People will be watching women's games who never watched before, because even though it's only two points, it's still the most exciting two points you can get."

In one game, Lynette seemed to have found the perfect moment to dunk. "When I led the break, even my teammates were yelling for me to throw it down (dunk)," Lynette recalls. "But I like to surprise people, so I just laid it in. But the next time I slowly ran down, then took off. I thought I had it." As it turned out, the ball bounced off the rim.

Before a 1980 college tournament, Lynette demonstrated her dunking skills in front of Madison Square Garden in New York City.

In 1981, Lynette was named the best female player in America. It's no wonder then, that the Globetrotters later chose her as their first female player.

THE FINEST FEMALE PLAYER IN AMERICA

For her senior season, Lynette averaged 24.5 points and 11.8 rebounds a game. The Lady Jayhawks ended the season with a 27-5 record. They made their best show ever in the AIAW tournament before bowing to UCLA, 73-71.

Lynette finished her college career with 3,649 points and 1,734 rebounds. She also had 141 blocked shots, 505 assists, and 537 steals. Each year, she had led the nation in some category (points, rebounds, or steals).

After the season, Street and Smith named Woodard as Co-Player of the Year. She won the Broderick Cup. She became only the second woman ever to be a Kodak All-American four years in a row. She was an Academic All-American for her second straight year. And, she was the first woman ever to be given the NCAA Top Five Award.

For her efforts, Lynette also earned the Wade Trophy, given each year to America's finest female player.

"For one person to be selected from so many gifted athletes is a treasure to behold," she said. "I thank God he allowed me to be accepted. I worked hard."

LYNETTE GOES TO ITALY

Even with all of her records, Lynette faced an uncertain future after graduation. The 1984 Olympics were three years away. The ill-fated Woman's Professional Basket-

Coaching wasn't what Lynette wanted. She loved to play basketball, as is shown by the look on her face during a Globetrotters game.

ball League was almost out of business. And while the door was open for Lynette to become a coach, she wasn't really ready to quit playing. "I love the game so much I

want to keep playing," she said. "I don't want to coach —
it would be sad if I had to stop playing."

Lynette found another way to stay active in the game.

Travelling by bus is a way of life for most basketball players.

She joined a basketball league in Italy. In the Italian League, Lynette earned enough money to live. At the same time, she was still an amateur. This meant Lynette

could get paid and still compete in the 1984 Olympics.

Playing in Italy had its benefits. Lynette was very big with the fans. Her 31 point average led the league. Still, it

Players who live together have to get along with each other. Lynette credits her time in Italy with making her a better person.

was difficult being so far from home.

"I thought when I first got there, 'Lord, what have I done,' " Lynette says. "I cried a lot at night."

"I had to really search inside. I had been in a structure all my life and I was out for the first time and here I was standing in this strange land."

In the end, Lynette came out of it as a stronger person. "I think it really helped me grow as a person," she says. "I learned to appreciate many things. Even though it was difficult, deep down in my heart I'm really grateful for the experience."

WOMAN OF THE YEAR

In 1982, Lynette accepted a coaching position at Kansas University. She wasn't ready to give up playing, but she had a lot of ideas she wanted to share.

"I know what it takes to get to the top," she said. "I've been there, and I understand what others are going through.

"Coach Washington never told us to do anything she wouldn't do herself. When we'd run, she'd run. When we would shoot, she'd shoot, too. I think that's important."

More than anything, Lynette wanted to help other young, gifted, female athletes believe in themselves. "It's mind over matter," she says. "If I see something done, then there's no doubt in my mind I can do it, too. It thrills me to be able to give that to other players."

As usual, Lynette still found time to support good causes. She started a Big Brother-Big Sister program on the KU campus. She worked for the Superkids program on behalf of the American Lung Association. She also gave time to support wheelchair-bound children.

In 1982, the NAACP honored Lynette for her public service. She was named as the Woman of the Year.

In 1982, and again in 1985, Lynette was named
Women of the Year by the NAACP.

Lynette worried about being too old to play well in 1984. She doesn't worry about that anymore, even when playing against much larger men!

THE 1984 OLYMPICS

In April of 1984, Lynette was invited to try out for the U.S. women's Olympic basketball team. Of the 107 hopefuls, the twenty-six-year old Woodard was one of the

oldest. She hadn't played college ball in over three years.
Some wondered if the game she helped put "on the map"
hadn't passed her by.

At Globetrotters' games, Lynette is introduced as a member of the 1984 Olympic team.

Woodard quickly put any doubts about her age aside. She not only made the U.S. team, but was named as co-captain. In the opening game in Los Angeles, Woodard scored 11 points and had 6 rebounds in a 83-55 win over Yugoslavia. In the second game, Lynette upped her scoring total to 15, with a 91-55 win over China.

After their third one-sided game in a row, an 89-68 win over Australia, U.S. hopes for a gold medal really began to soar. Another win — by 37 points — over Korea, 84-47, put the U.S. team only one game away from the gold medal.

The U.S. faced South Korea in the title game. For a

while, it was very close. After a 16-2 surge, however, the U.S. had a fifteen point lead. The final score was 85-55, in favor of the U.S. "It's a great feeling to have won the gold," Lynette said proudly after the game.

BRINGING HOME THE GOLD

After the Olympics, Lynette returned to Wichita for a special homecoming. The ceremony was held at Wichita North High School. Duane Schmidt, Marian Washington, old friends, and family all attended. Lynette, whose college jersey was now in the Basketball Hall of Fame in New York, stood in the middle of it all. She wore her Olympic warm-up suit and the Olympic gold medal. When she was introduced, she got a huge cheer.

"I've been around the world playing basketball," she said, smiling. "But it feels really good to be back home. This is the house of the Redskins. We're number one!"

A standing ovation told Lynette who was number one in the minds of the students. Of all who had gone on from Wichita North, none had gone further than Lynette Woodard. The students listened intently as Lynette told them that they, too, should reach for the stars.

"The biggest thing to remember," she said, "Is that you have to take the little steps before you can take the big ones." And it wasn't long before the Globetrotters asked her to try out. The rest is now history!

*In early 1985, Lynette's dream came true — she was a
Globetrotter!*

People of all ages like to hear about Lynette's experiences.

There are times when even a star like Lynette has to sit on the bench!

LYNETTE WOODARD'S COLLEGE STATISTICS

Kansas University Lady Jayhawks

Year	Points (Avg.)	Rebounds (Avg.)	Assts.	Steals	Blocks
1977-78	830 (25.2)	490 (14.8)	47	15	7
1978-79	1,177 (31.7)	545 (14.3)	97	193	56
1979-80	881 (23.8)	389 (10.5)	165	177	35
1980-81	761 (24.5)	310 (11.8)	196	152	43
Totals	3,649 (26.3)	1,734 (12.8)	505	537	141

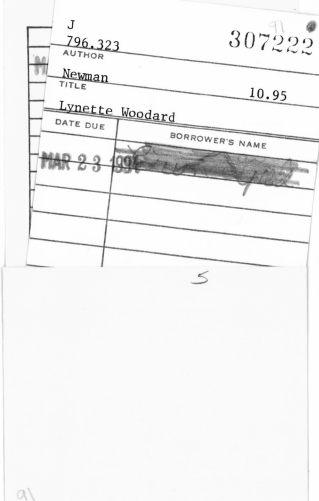